DONCASTER HIS

There could be some truth in it.

Tales from around Doncaster

- Ch 1 - Introduction.
- Ch 2 - A woman's work.... - a Warmsworth Farmer.
- Ch 3 - Sprotbrough Beware! - Cromwell is about.
- Ch 4 - The White Greyhound of Edlington.
- Ch 5 - Chinese whispers V the facts - the Cat and Man of Barnburgh.
- Ch 6 - A brief history of Scawthorpe.
- Ch 7 - Bell Pond, the story behind the name (Sprotbrough).
- Ch 8 - Doncaster Floods, the joys and perils of living in the Don valley.
- Ch 9 - Portland Place, Doncaster.
- Ch 10 - Bowers Fold, Doncaster.
- Ch 11 - French Gate, Doncaster.
- Ch 12 - The Future, as of 91 years ago.

DONCASTER HISTORY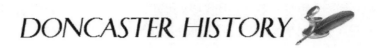

Introduction

Doncaster, in South Yorkshire, England is a traditional market town that, like every other town in the United Kingdom, is attempting to evolve into a 21st century, viable, self supporting entity. While it is essential to make progress to survive, it is also vital that we don't forget where we came from. Busy lives and forward thinkers help the populace to become distracted from their roots. The purpose of this small publication is to draw attention to just a handful of stories from the area covering the last 2 to 3 hundred years, to highlight the fact that we have been around as an important town for quite some time now, and to attempt to encourage those that are interested enough to delve into the past and see for themselves what a wonderful, 'history steeped' place we live in.

Doncaster's heritage has been traced back into pre-history, long before the Roman's were even thought of, and it has continued to be a viable settling place through Roman, Saxon, Norman, Plantagenet, Tudor, and Elizabethan times, and on into the Restoration, Georgian, Victorian and Post War era's.

With all this history and heritage come a great deal of documentation and it is these written records that I enjoy studying the most. Facts and figures, points of law, changes in legislation, or just simple diaries, have become my favoured method of researching our past. I have acquired the ability to form vivid mental pictures of our ancestors from these documents and I hope that my style of writing allows you to do the same.

This publication evolves out of my incredibly popular internet based project simply entitled, 'Doncaster History' (www.doncasterhistory.co.uk). After reading this short booklet, please visit the web site where you will find a wealth of facts, information, and stories, always on a Doncaster theme. The whole resource is free and I sincerely hope you will find it fascinating.

Enjoy this book but more importantly, **enjoy your heritage.**

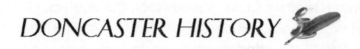

DONCASTER HISTORY

A Woman's Work...

Elizabeth Crawshaw was born in 1776 in Yorkshire. She married her husband John who was 5 years her senior and by the year 1799 and at the age of just 23, she was a farmer of over 150 acres at Warmsworth.

My wife often likes to point out the various hardships she endures as she juggles being a mum, a wife, a house-wife and a full time employee. I try not to argue with her on this as 12 years of experience has taught me to bow to her superior knowledge on the subject.

Let us think though, for a few paragraphs, about the workload of Elizabeth Crawshaw and how she managed to successfully run a farm and a family in the early 1800s.

The land that Elizabeth farmed was not her own. She rented it from William Battie-Wrightson Esq. As with all landlords, occasionally there would be rent increases and for this to be administered fairly, a valuation of the property had to take place. One such valuation was undertaken in 1799 commissioned by Battie-Wrightson and is a fantastic insight into the extent of Elizabeth's responsibilities. As landlord, he leased out a total of four farms in Warmsworth. Elizabeth's farm was one of the larger estates and consisted of Croft, Pickhill, Lime Kiln Close, Low West Yard, Spittle Yard and Common, Ridding Close, Wood Nook Close, Beck Close, Great Wood Nook, Glebe in Turnpike Close, Burr Flatt, Middle Field, Don Field, and Church Field, to name just some of it. The whole estate was surveyed at 150 acres, 1 rood, 28 perches (or today, 150.425 acres) and the yearly rental value was £151 4s 0d (or approximately £9000).

Some of the place names that are listed above are still hinted at today with road names such as Glebe Street, Common Lane, and Croft Road. Middle Field is now the site of the huge Warmsworth quarry just off the A630 Sheffield Road, and Church Field is now the extensive housing estate which has Tenter Lane as its spine.

It is unclear to me without further research exactly where Elizabeth lived although the survey does make mention of a

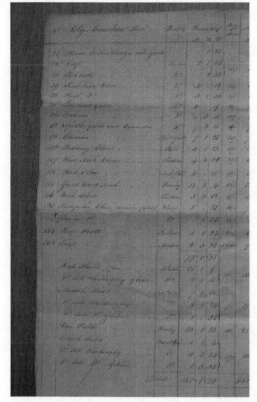

rather large house with outbuildings and a yard. Under closer scrutiny I would guess that the area immediately surrounding Warmsworth Hall was its location, one of the reasons being, that Lime Kilns are mentioned and there were such kilns on land adjacent to the Warmsworth Hall around this time.

Certain restrictions were placed on the lease and one such is as follows:

"Elizabeth Crawshaw should be allowed to have no more than 24 acres of enclosed land in tillage (or ploughed) at one time, which will complete a regular round of fallow (uncultivated) with the field lands. She may change the other enclosed land by taking up and seeding down, but should not plough High and Low West Yard, Lime Kiln Close, Crofts, and the Don Ings".

She also had Tithes to pay, on top of her rent which amounted to somewhere in the region of £30 (£1,700) per year.

Later in life, she and her husband John, although still living in Warmsworth, had handed the running of the farm over to their

Daughter, also called Elizabeth. This Elizabeth was a single parent to Edward age 14, Eliza age 13, Catherine age 10, and Jessy age 7. She did have help from her Father (now 70 years of age!) and from 3 female and 3 male servants, all of whom are listed in the 1841 census, a luxury that my wife wishes for from time to time.

As we try to imagine farming in those times, we think of horse-drawn ploughs and jolly plough boys taking for lunch of bread and cheese under the shade of a stately oak tree, warm summer days in the great Yorkshire countryside. This couldn't

be further from the truth. It was a life of hardship and toil as Elizabeth's father would tell us if he were here now.

There are those of us that complain from time to time at the thought of retirement age increasing and of the responsibilities that go hand in hand with providing for our families but, spare a thought for Elizabeth and her Father,

John. While ever there was breath in their bodies and they were physically able, they worked the land in Warmsworth in order to put bread on the table for their families.

Sprotbrough Beware!

On 25th April, 1599, a baby boy was born to middle gentry parents in Huntingdon, Cambridgeshire. The child was christened Oliver Cromwell. His family had once been one of the wealthiest in the county although, by now they ranked closer to the bottom when compared with their peers. That said, Oliver had inherited money and lands from his now deceased Father and Uncle and was able to gain a top education at grammar school followed by Cambridge University.

After his schooling he made money through farming and by charging rents on his land. His money had to stretch quite far though, as he had a wife and eight children to support along with his widowed Mother. He dabbled with politics but was never very influential, until, that is, the English Civil War 'kicked off'. In 1640 he became an MP for Cambridge and raised troops for the cause in 1642. He fought on the side of the Roundheads, or parliamentarians, against the Crown. His success in battle saw him climbing the career ladder as fast as lightning until he became commander of the entire army. He overthrew the Stuart Monarchy by having Charles I tried and executed in January, 1649. By July, 1650, he was leading his army north to crush Scotland, then over the sea to subdue Ireland and up and down the British Isles taking on every Royalist army that tried to stand in his way.

Understandably, people were afraid of Cromwell's presence in their town, so that in August 1651 when he passed through Doncaster, extreme caution was required.

At Sprotbrough Hall, lived Sir Godfrey Copley, who had control over who crossed the Don River in the gorge as he owned and ran the ferry. The Ferryboat Inn, now the Boat Inn, stood on the banks and at the boarding point for it.

Although Cromwell marched into Doncaster closer to town, where the river was bridged, he could have quite possibly opted to cross the river in Sprotbrough. Because of this possibility, Sir Godfrey received a letter from his brother-in-law

Darcy Wentworth along with other friends, urging him to undertake certain measures to ensure his and his family's safety at this volatile time.

The letter went as follows (spelling errors and all):

"*Esteemed Sir,*

'*Such is the condition of our cuntrie at present as requires care to be taken as passingers; And there beeinge a by way over your ferry roed thought fit to de?so?e you would be pleased to command that your ferry boate to be locked up that there be noe passidge for frind or strangers feet untill you have further notice that there may be passidge when safetie werest.*'

Septeme 7ᵗʰ 1651

> *Your family and ser[vants]*
>
> *Dar Wentworth*
>
> *John Copley*
>
> *???*
>
> *????????*
>
> *G. Byan*"

Good cousin be carefull whome ye entertaine for ye danger is greate.

The letter is of a serious nature and carries a strong message. 'Lock up your Ferryboat to both friends and strangers' and be careful who you have round for tea!

It would be 250 years before the Copley's provided a bridge at this point. It came in the form of a toll bridge. By now, the Civil War was ancient history and on the adjacent bank of the Don stood the thriving quarrying community of Levitt Hagg. Today lower Sprotbrough is one of the most picturesque corners of Doncaster with its quaint pub by the canal and its nature reserve providing a haven for wildlife and a gateway to the Pennines beyond. Sprotbrough can rest easy again as the marauding armies have long since vanished. The 'danger' is no longer 'greate' for us.

The White Greyhound of Edlington.

Around 350 years ago in Edlington, lived an Irish nobleman by the name of Viscount Robert Molesworth the 1st, of Swords. Swords was and is a town to the north of Dublin, Ireland. The Viscount came to England through his work as an MP for the West Riding of Yorkshire (a constituency now known as Don Valley) and settled at Edlington wood. His property was called Blow Hall Manor which, unfortunately, is no longer with us. I found the following extract in a book from 1837 entitled 'The English Counties Delineated - by Thomas Moule, it reads: "In Edlington wood is Blow Hall, a conical pile of un-hewn stones and a double dyke. [Surrounded by] a bank of earth and stone about three feet in height and as many in breadth which may be traced the whole extent of the wood in a straight line from north-west to south-east...."

He lived at the Hall with his wife, Lady Letitia Molesworth; his children, and his faithful 'snow-white' Greyhound.

Robert was said to have been extremely close to his canine companion so that they were rarely apart, enjoying regular excursions between London, Ireland, and Edlington. Legend dictates that the trusted Greyhound one day went above the call of duty, the story of which goes this way:

Viscount Molesworth was busy working in the gardens of his Edlington estate, when 'nature called' he started to make his way to the outside toilet. The dog was not keen on the idea and, using his teeth, clamped onto his masters tailcoat in order to dissuade him. The Viscount, on making a second attempt, was met with the same response from the hound. Surprised by this, Robert ordered one of his gardeners to go ahead to the loo to check that all was well. On opening the door he was immediately shot dead by a villain who had been hiding in there, most probably lying in wait for darkness so as to rob the house when all were sleeping.

This act of supreme protection forged an unbreakable bond between dog and master. Some years later, on the death of the Greyhound, Robert erected a fine monument under a yew tree in the grounds of Blow Hall Manor. The monument took the shape of an urn resting on a square pedestal, the front of which carried a carving of the faithful dog on white marble. There was also an inscription in Latin, which when translated, read:

"Stay traveller, nor wonder that a lamented dog is thus interred with funeral honour. But ah, what a dog! His beautiful form and snow-white colour, pleasing manners and sporting playfulness, affection, obedience, and fidelity, made him the delight of his master. To whose side he closely adhered, with his eager companions of the chase. He delighted in attending him. Whenever the mind of his lord was depressed, he would assume fresh spirit and animation. A master, not ungrateful for his merits, has here in tears deposited his remains in this marble urn, in the year 1714."

The memory of this legend being passed down from generation to generation led to there being a street (Blow Hall Crescent) and a public house named after the tale, but the pub has been replaced with a new development and the houses on the street demolished.

I have been told that the monument is still in existence but I do not know its exact location.

Chinese Whispers V the Facts

When I think of the village of Barnburgh, I think - 'Cat and Man'. I would be very surprised if you haven't heard the tale of Percival Cresacre and the wildcat. Legend has it that Cresacre was riding on horseback and wrestling with a large wild cat right up to the Church. In the end they killed each other at the same time and the blood still stains the church steps. It seems to me that this story has stuck to the village like glue much the same as the 'Hickleton Skulls' and 'Sir Walter Scott and Sprotbrough'.

Legends are fantastic little pieces of history based on nothing but hearsay. The Cat and Man legend is a fantastic example of a cross between Chinese whispers and a fisherman describing how big his catch was. I wouldn't at all be surprised if the original story went something like this:

"Percy was riding home one night when Mrs Smith's moggy startled his horse and caused it to rear up. Percy was thrown to the ground and sprained his ankle, THE END"

Personally, I much prefer to delve into the sort of history that is based on the facts and there is a lesser known story from

Barnburgh which is far more factual. It concerns the 'More' family.

That part of the Cat and Man tale which is true is the family name. The Cresacres did indeed inhabit Barnburgh from 1281 as the family had moved to England to be with their King, William the Conqueror. The Cresacres were the Lords of Manor of Barnburgh right up until 1528 when, because of a distinct lack of male heirs, Annie Cressacre, who had inherited the estate in 1512, was married to John More at the age of 18.

John was the son of the famous Sir Thomas More, Henry VIII's trusted chancellor, who, like many of his closest advisors and family, met his doom at the Kings hand. He had earned the trust of the King over a great many years so that by 1517 he was instrumental in quelling a London uprising against foreigners. In 1518 he became a member of the Privy Council and was knighted in 1521. He was made Speaker of the House of Commons in 1523 and Chancellor of the Duchy of Lancaster in 1525. He stood up to the King in 1527 when he refused to endorse his plans to divorce Katherine of Aragon, however, despite this rather large difference of opinion he was still trusted enough to be made Lord Chancellor of all England in 1529.

Despite earning the highest of regard from King Henry it did not end well for Sir Thomas, as, when it started to go wrong, his fall from grace happened quickly. By 1532 he had resign through ill health, although the true reason was probably more to do with the Kings desire to break from Rome and create his own Church of England. He refused to attend the coronation of Anne Boleyn in 1533 which came to King Henry's notice. From that point on, Henry had it in for him and he was implicated in all manner of foul deeds. He was eventually imprisoned in the Tower of London where he was tried and found guilty of treason for which charge he was beheaded on 6th July, 1635.

Annie Cresacre's husband, the afore-mentioned John More was a Catholic, just like his father Sir Thomas. This meant that they had to be secretive about their religion and there was even a Priest Hole in Barnburgh Hall.
The More's went on to live at Barnburgh Hall and to be Lords of the manor until 1822. After that time, the fine country residence passed through various hand until eventually, the Coal Board, who were in residence at the time, decided it was suffering from terrible mining subsidence and so had to be demolished in the interest of public safety. It has since been speculated that the reason given for the demolition was nothing more than an elaborate excuse to get rid of a building that was becoming increasingly more costly to run and repair.

A brief History of Scawthorpe

Being from Scawthorpe myself, it probably comes as no surprise to you that I have an interest in the history of the village. You would be forgiven for thinking that Scawthorpe is a 20th century creation as; at one time the village was a small (very small) hamlet in the bigger estate of Bentley and Arksey. When the coal mine came to Bentley in 1905 the immediate and surrounding areas were ripe for development as a massive influx of workers created the urgent need for affordable housing. Good sized, 3 bedroom houses were built by the Doncaster Corporation and the NCB.

What was Scawthorpe like before this transformation?

Slicing through the top most part of Scawthorpe and forming the boundary between itself and Sunnyfields is York Road.

This busy link road runs parallel and approximately 500 yards from the 'Roman Ridge', part of the Great North Road which was constructed by the Romans. Being in such close proximity to such an important trading route, Scawthorpe must have seen many travellers throughout the centuries.

When William the Conqueror came to England in 1066, one of his important supporters, a certain Nigel Fossard was rewarded for his service to the king in his battle against Harold. Part of his award was lands in this area; one of those manors was that of Arksey. Scawthorpe and Bentley came under the umbrella of Arksey and Fossard placed his stamp on the area by building fortified manor houses. One of these houses was Radcliffe Moat, a motte and bailey castle between Scawthorpe and Bentley (now intersected by the York railway line), the other, and Radcliffe's predecessor, was the scheduled ancient monument at Castle Hills.

The monument comprised a 4-5m high motte with a kidney-shaped inner bailey to the north and a sub-rectangular outer bailey to the east. The inner bailey was approximately 30m across and the outer bailey approximately 70m x 40m. On the west side, between the motte and inner bailey, a 2m high oval mound formed the end of the rampart circling the motte to the south west and has since been interpreted as a defended approach to the monument.

The complexity of the earthworks suggests that it was a monument of some importance. Certainly it commanded the manor of Langthwaite (later Hangthwaite), one of six held by Nigel Fossard in 1086 from the Count of Mortain. The de Langthwaites seem to have become an important family, whose name appears in many northern documents. It was in the later medieval period that the manor was moved approximately 300m east to Radcliffe.

The immediate area was essentially a medium sized village and recent finds in the soil adjoining the castle mounds strongly suggest this to be case.

Jumping forward 2-3 hundred years brings us to the time of the Cooke's of Wheatley. The Cooke family became the Lords of the Manor of Arksey. This manor contained a number of smaller hamlets namely, Almholme, Bodles, Doncaster-Bridgend, Scawthorpe, Shaftholme, and Stockbridge. By the time of the 1871 census, there was only one residence recorded in Scawthorpe. There was no address listed, the entry simply calls the building, a farm, Scawthorpe. Living there was the Farmer and his Wife, a Mr and Mrs Monton, their 2 children Ernest and Mona, a female servant named Elizabeth Welbnom (possible mis-spelling), and 3 farm labourers all with the same Christian name, Thomas Millers, Thomas Thorpe, and Thomas Exley, the farmer obviously liked the name Tom!

By the 1920's, the village and surrounding area was described this way by Eric Higton of the nearby mining village of Highfields:

"As with Sprotbrough Lane, there were no building except farm properties on Castle Hills Lane and Green Lane (which boasted a fishpond where it joined the main road, and was known locally as fishpond lane). On the left hand side of the track as it neared the top of the rise opposite Jossey Lane stood Scawthorpe Hall with its three lodges, the centre one of which stood empty for some time; the windows boarded up. Locally, it was reputed to be haunted."

By 1986, such was the necessity to build, build, build more housing for the mine workers, the description was somewhat different:

"Just 2.5 miles north-west of Doncaster beside the old Great North Road lies Scawthorpe a residential area built in the

1920's with private houses, Coal Board and Council properties. Many coal miners and their families live in this community. There are also bungalows and flats for the elderly and a home for the disabled. In Scawthorpe there is not much traffic and it is quite a quiet place. There is a group of basic shops, a clinic and a doctor's surgery. There is also a working men's club, a pub, two churches and a library. Five schools serve the area catering for every age group. Scawthorpe estate is laid out in geometric patterns, with small green spaces where children can play. There is some light industry and on two sides it is surrounded by farm land."

Bell Pond – the story behind the name

In 1850, John George Fardell, Rector of Sprotbrough writes – "It possesses little in the way of picturesque beauty – little of those attractions which mark the character of the brook-stream, sauntering through all pleasant places, seeking out happy nooks and peaceful recesses. But Bell Pond is the ancient of days, and possesses its peculiar history and its peculiar associations."

Where is Bell Pond I hear you ask? On foot, it can be reached following this route. Taking the road between the Goldsmith centre and Sprotbrough Fish Bar, walk under the railway bridge and down into the tiny hamlet of Newton, at the junction, turn right and follow the Don navigation for about 1 mile. From the flood defence bank that you now find yourself on, Bell bond is on your right.

From the ground it is quite impossible to see its shape properly but from the air it possesses the form of what can only be described as a horse-shoe. Although peaceful and serene today, providing a haven for an abundance of wildlife and a much needed watering hole for the grazing sheep, the pond hides a much sinister past and if the imagination is loosened for a moment while I relay this story, you may well feel differently about the scene from here-on in.

Fardell continues – "Its character now is distinctly marked. It is without form, if not void; amid a confusion of shapes; mysterious, amid a brood of mysteries. Its waters know no current – they are mute, motionless, death-like, fearful; they are deep and appalling, but contain the soul of hidden mysteries; they are surrounded by a host of goodly trees, which have undergone no change from generation to generation; they are peculiar in their character; they are strangers among strangers, yet faithful to their purpose; they are aged among the aged, yet bid defiance to storm or hurricane; they are safely anchored to the banks by countless cables, knarled and twisted and tough. Indeed the pond possesses the same reputation as a haunted house; and therefore the inference may be drawn that some historic deed, some adventure, some misfortune, is associated with Bell Pond".

The Rector paints a pretty bleak picture of what we now see as a pleasant expanse of water in a quiet and unspoilt corner of Sprotbrough. He is setting the scene for a tale of love found and lost, desertion, isolation, ostracism, loneliness, and death.

He goes on – "In the year 1685, immediately after the revocation of the edict of Nantes, upwards of 80,000 individuals sought a spot of refuge in this country. Among this body of refugees was the remnant of an ancient family of the name of Dumas, consisting of only two individuals, Madame Dumas and her only daughter, Isabelle. Madame Dumas died and Isabelle was left alone in the world. She was adorned with surpassing beauty and loveliness. She enchained all hearts by her personal charms, but more by her unostentatious goodness, unsullied purity and true female dignity. Unfortunately for her, she formed an attachment to the youngest son of an old Catholic family, an offshoot of one of the ancient Catholic Nobility.

The passion was mutual, and after a severe trial she was induced to renounce her Protestant belief and to embrace the Roman faith. The adoption of this step entailed upon her the loss of all her old friends; and as calamities never come single handed, her lover, who then was a commander in the Royal Navy, lost his life in an attack off Sandwich with a body of smuggling Hollanders.

Thus having lost everything, and being cut off from all hope for the future, she very happily obtained a refuge in a family then resident at Sprotbrough, a distant branch; it was surmised, of the De Maulays, of Hexthorpe. But the heart of Isabelle was stricken with an incurable blight. Her days were the days of gloom and despondency – her nights the nights of sadness and anguish.

She wandered alone through the intricacies of what was then called Conisbrough forest, climbed the barren heights of Cadeby, or lingered alone in the depths of the valley below. Her foster friends pitied her fate, and tried to soothe her feelings by the words and deeds on consolation and comfort; yet, on the strength and nobleness of her mind they placed the fullest confidence.

At length she was missing; instant search was made for her in every conceivable direction, and by every available means.

'Twas all in vain. In the course of a short time, however, the secret was laid open. She had drowned herself in the pond not too far from Sprotbrough. Her corpse was taken from its hiding place and immediately interred, without inscription or headstone, in the churchyard of Sprotbrough.

From that mournful period these dark waters bore the name of Isabelle Pond, which has since been corrupted into Bell Pond".

Doncaster Floods

The joys and perils of living in the Don valley

By the year 1700 Marshgate was made up of just 4 houses. The river Cheswold dissected a part of it and was said to be 'as nature had left it'. In 1735 there was an increase of 7 properties, and by the 1760s there was a considerable increase in the number of properties there. Back then, much the same as today, Marshgate was out on a limb. From the recent floods which engulfed town end Bentley, parts of Sprotbrough, together with Marshgate we can see that little much has changed through the centuries regarding its vulnerability given its close proximity to the main water courses in town.

Hatfield writes, in his Historical Notices of Doncaster – 1868, "Now and then the accumulated waters have laid waste the fairest lands and prostrated the works of man". He recalls with vivid memories "the alarming disaster of February 8th, 1861" where "the tide overflowed the banks of the river with an irresistible force; and, as if impatient of restraint, broke through bridges, snapped asunder gates and palings, threw back the increasing streams from ancient drains and water courses, swept itself in solemn majesty over opposing obstacles, chafed, fretted, and roared through bridge and culvert, stopped water wheels and mill wheels, rushed into cellars of cottages, and crept upstairs to the house apartments, dashed through smaller tenements, out of the way nooks and corners, threw into utter confusion the occupiers of farm homesteads, disturbed beasts in their sheds, alarmed fowls on their perches, filled saw pits, and timber floated about like mere toys, deluged village lanes and byeways, ever pressing onwards in its destructive career; at one fell swoop, game of all kinds, from the timid hare to the bright plumed pheasant were carried away regardless of the preserver; at length, tired and disappointed, the turbulent waters rolled backwards, and places hitherto free were turned upside down; but again returning with another violent effort to escape dashed forward, carrying death and terror in its path, until it found vent in the tidal waters of the Humber".

Lady Pitts Bridge was constructed by Joseph Lockwood and is a rather grand looking series of arches spanning over 100 yards. It would appear, to the untrained eye, to be a classic case of over-engineering on Lockwood's part, as the water it bridges is a mere ditch measuring about 3 feet wide. Do not be fooled! The trickle becomes a torrent in times of flood as the Don Navigation overflows at Crimpsall under (and sometimes over) the Sprotbrough road, behind the houses of Northfield road and on towards Morrisons supermarket. On November 20th, 1791, Lady Pitts Bridge successfully resisted the pressure of such a torrent. Part of one of the arches was thrown to the ground but the bridge remained intact. On the low lands around it the waters settled at a depth of 6 feet allowing boats to sail across them with ease. The boats were used to ferry the milkmen, butchers, and bakers from house to house, making their deliveries through the upstairs windows. One Bentley farmer lost "three score of fine sheep" on that fateful day.

In a similar flood in the summer of 1828 the waters of the Cheswold rose rapidly on the morning of Sunday 13th July. Farm workers hurriedly attempted to rescue the hay in Crimpsall. A number of labourers were employed during the whole of that day, in "attempting to hinder the progress of the water, by raising the western bank from the foundry near the Mill Bridge to Newton. It continued to swell, and on Monday, the northern bank of the Mill Dyke gave way. The efforts to remedy this breach were fruitless; and the Ings of Bentley and Arksey became deluged". The area of Crimpsall where only 3 days before had seen the rescue of the hay, now became a boating marina for the pleasure seekers of the town.

The water in Crimpsall, as viewed from Friar's Bridge, presented one unbroken, glassy surface. "The reflections of the rays of the glorious sun, the forms of the ever varying clouds, the willows which fringed the southern side and the trees along the line of the Cheswold exhibited a novel spectacle".

The flood waters in French Gate reached the Brown Cow public house. "At one period of the flood a curious sight was observed in the shape of what appeared to be a floating island drifting slowly with the stream. The water careering along in its unopposed course swept with it, in one compact body, a huge mass of earth, flags, sedges, and rushes from the pool at Arksey, and the moving island had all the appearance of *terra firma* as it glided down the flood".

The problems that occurred time after time down in Marshgate were caused, mainly because of the Newton Bank which reinforced the river bank from what is now St Marys Bridge to the Hamlet of Newton itself. It was always the bank on the Marshgate side that the waters breached, forever causing much devastation there, until that is, the flood of Saturday 6th August, 1846. A decision was made to let the banks fail on the Newton side for a change. Hatfield writes, "The Newton Bank, the main cause of the mischief, was cut, at all hazards, opposite the south end of the Black Pond. From thence it ran across Sprotbrough road, past Anchorage Farm, made its way beneath Willow Bridge on the Great North Road, and joined the swollen brook stream of the Boiling Basin at Cusworth Ponds to the south side of Bentley Bank, and so on to the tide-way at Thwaite House. The relief afforded to Marshgate was apparent. Crimpsall had the appearance of a large pool; and the long lines of light from the lamps at the Railway Station, and the public ones elsewhere, reflected from the scarcely rippled surface of the water, had a striking effect, while the distant roar of the river weir, and that of the rushing stream through the bank cutting, produced a picture rarely seen in this part of the country".

The men that were responsible for making the cut in Newton Bank did so without thought for their own safety. They also cared not for the consequences of such an act as; it was not their place to make such a decision. What was to be their fate?

"They were harassed and charged on the information of Benjamin Mangham, Lock Keeper, that they 'did, then and there, unlawfully, maliciously, and feloniously, break down, and cut down, a certain bank of a certain river, called the river Don, there situate, by means whereof certain lands were then and there overflowed and damaged, against the form of the statute in that case made and provided'. On Saturday August 28th, at the Town Hall, the case was heard before Richard Heber Wrightson, Esq. John William Sturges, Esq. Wm. Aldam, Esq. James Brown, Esq. Sir Isaac Morley, and Captain

Bower, and occupied nine columns of the supplement to the Doncaster Gazette of Sept 1st".

To cut a long story short, the bench decided that no further action would be taken against the men on the grounds that, the corporation probably should have stepped in themselves but failed to do so, and in addition, the bank was more than likely erected illegally in the first place anyway. The case against the men was dismissed. It was later found that the bank had been constructed higher than the floors of the houses in Marshgate which speaks for itself really; the flood waters would reach the doorstep of the dwellings before it breached Newton Bank.

In June 2007, the waters of the Don once again rose and breached the Newton Bank at Black Pond. The water began to seek out all its ancient ways and dry stream beds came back to life. Ponds appeared where fields should be and rivers flowed where roads should be. The route that the waters took in the middle 19th century was the exact same route that they took in 2007. This highlights to me the fact, that we are guests on this earth, we can try to change nature, we can attempt to re-route water courses and build houses on seemingly safe tracts of land, however, when nature needs an escape route, the best engineers in the land cannot stand in its path.

Portland Place

The 1816 Mayor of Doncaster, John Pearson Esq. owned what was referred to as 'garden ground' situated behind Spring Gardens in the town. The large tract of land, surrounded by a high wall, would have looked much the same as an oversized Victorian kitchen garden. Mr Pearson decided to sell off the land so that by 1825-26, William Hirst Esq., an architect, began to design the layout of a street.

Some of the land was purchased by Mr Benjamin Hammond, a Doncaster pawnbroker. A section of the land that he bought was later sold off to a Mrs Miles. She kept the land as 'garden ground'. It was situated close to Cleveland Street, and opposite the new Civic Quarter, multi-storey car park. It remained in this natural state until her death. The land was then purchased by a Mr Wood who decided to build on it, firstly by constructing 2 cottages on the frontage to Cleveland Street, followed by 4 tenements (or apartments) in Portland Place itself. Mr Hammond, on his land, built 'country-like' housing which became very sought after by a better class of society, raising the tone of the area in general, however, his increased wealth led enabled him to construct more 'affordable housing' there which attracted a lower class of tenant. This influx of lower-class individuals had the effect of driving out the well-to-do and lowering the general tone. Opposite Mr Hammond's dwellings, yet another landlord, one Mr Tummond, built 4 cottages, one of which was turned into a shop. The above named individuals now owned the majority of the area and so were legally entitled to rename it. Previously it had been known as Bird-in-hand-yard and latterly, Elbow Street due to its crookedness, but now it was to be known as Portland Place.

In 1832, Mr Tummond sold an allotment to a Mr Charles Siddall, a builder, who then erected six cottages on the site, 2 at the front and 4 behind. At the death of Mr Tummond, Mr Edward Burton, Tailor and Draper, father of Mr W. T. Burton of 'Plant & Burton Drapers, Baxter Gate, came into possession along with the six other cottages.

Over time, the properties changed hands and other building were erected on the site until, by 1868, Portland Place was made up of about 40 separate dwellings, the majority of them being owned by the Hammond family. Mr Benjamin Hammond had died in the Horse Fair (now Waterdale) was buried in the Parish Churchyard (The Minster) May 11th, 1853, has a tablet near to the south wall of St. Georges Church which reads, "Here lie interred the remains of Wm James, son of Wm and Elizabeth Hammond, who departed this life Aug 19th, 1787, in the fourth year of his age. Also, the remains of the above named Wm Hammond, who departed this life the 28th day of June, 1795, in the 49th year of his age, and of the said Elizabeth Hammond, who departed this life the 28th July, 1822, in the 58th year of her age, testifying their dependence on Jesus Christ, the foundation of their life. Also, near this place are interred Josias and Henry Hammond, children of the above, who died in infancy".

Mr Hammond was for many years an extensive tea dealer, and according to the announcement, his death took place on, "Sunday, after a tedious indisposition (long illness). Deservedly respected". He had lived at number 18, Hall Gate.

Bowers Fold

This ancient part of the town was, and still is the link between two streets, namely, Silver Street and Market Place. The fold used to link Silver Street with New Street, but like many of our old streets, New Street is no longer with us. It takes its name from Mr John Bower who was an Alderman of Doncaster in the 16th century.

The following extract is taken from Hatfield's Historical Notices and reads:

"The Bower-fold garden is mentioned in an indenture tripartite (three part contract), made the fifth day of August in the eighth year of the reign of Lady Ann, by the Grace of God, of Great Britain and Ireland, Queen Defender of the faith **A.D. 1709**, between Kingston Futcher, of Fisherton, Anger, in the county of Wiltshire, and Mary, his wife, and heir of Edward Sansome, late of Doncaster, in the county of York, Coachmaker, deceased, and Kingston Futcher and Edward Futcher, sons of the said Kingston Futcher, by the said Mary, his wife, of the first part; and John Cowley, jun. of Doncaster aforesaid, gent. of the second part; and Edward Holliday of the same place, gent. of the third part, witnesseth that the said Kingston Futcher, and Mary, his said wife, Kingston Futcher, jun. and Edward Futcher for, and in consideration of, the sum of twenty one pounds and ten shillings of current money of Great Britain, to them in hand paid by the said John Cowley before the execution hereof, doth grant, alienate, bargain, sell, enfeoff (land in exchange for a pledge of service), release, and confirm unto the said John Cowley, for ever, **all that orchard, or garden,with the appurtenances, lying, and being in Doncaster, near unto a certain place there, called the Bower Fold, now in the possession of the said John Cowley, and late in possession of Francis Earnshaw, containing, by estimation one rood of land (¼ acre),** be the same more or less, and was formerly the inheritance of Matthew Snowsell, deceased".

According to Mr William Sheardown, twice Mayor of Doncaster in the 1830's, 'Bower Fold was also referred to as Boar Fold during the late 1700's, and was never so closed in as it appears today', in fact, it resembled what we would now call a 'cul-de-sac' and was a continuation of Silver Street set in tranquil grounds. Another eye-witness account from 1777 describes it this way: 'This passage was not narrow or confined, open ground contributed to the health and pleasure of the cottagers. Although gardens faced the opening, and are included in Bower Fold, they formed a part of Silver Street. Mr Ashton's garden extended to one rood (¼ acre), and another nearly of the same dimensions. Mr John Britain and Mr John Halliday also had one, at the annual rateable value of fifteen shillings each. Besides were small dwelling houses tenanted by John Green, Thomas Morritt, and Thomas Barnes'.

It seems that Bowers Fold was a little part of the countryside right in the centre of a town. The large gardens and the idyllic setting made the Bower Fold a pleasure to live in. Quaint cottages with large sprawling gardens and orchards.

A far cry from what we see today as upwards of 15 shops and 2 public houses are crammed in to the now tiny space. I wouldn't like to live there and I doubt, if one or two of the former residents from the 1700's were to pay it a visit, whether they would either.

French Gate

French gate was once part of the 'inner sanctum' of Doncaster. In 1194 the Doncaster township acquired a 19ft wide by 8ft deep defensive ditch (known as the Bardyke) in response to tension between Royalty and the Church. Prince John had supporters who had taken over Tickhill Castle which stimulated the Archbishop of York (King Richard's half brother), in his role as Sheriff of Yorkshire, to garrison 180 soldiers in Doncaster for 40 days. Remains of this ditch have since been found lying beneath Factory lane (Sunny Bar), and Cleveland street. A bar would have been the name for the points at which the ditch could be crossed.

The township within the dyke developed a street line along French gate (whose name hints at the link to our Norman invaders), with long and thin house and garden plots built end on to the street. The settlement would be entered via one of the many gates or bars, i.e. Sunny Bar, Marsh gate, French gate, and St. Sepulchre gate.

One tenement (or multi-family dwelling) was described in 1316 this way:

"Sicut jacet inter Messuaguim Reginaldi de Darthington ex una parte et Messuaguim Thomoe de Fledburgh ex altera parte cujus unum caput buttat super vicum Franciscum, &c."

"And which is situate between the messuage of Reginald de Darthington on the one side and the messuage of Thomas de Fledburgh on the other, so that one end abutts upon Francis (French) street."

Thomas de Fledburgh was a well thought of man in these parts, he must have been or why else would Roger, the Parson of Doncaster grant him this "messuage with the outbuildings" on what is now called French gate. Fledburgh was a loyal supporter of King Edward II so that while the King was busy fighting battles in the north of England, Thomas, who had a flock of his own, was hurriedly gathering his followers together to pay homage to the King and his great deeds. King Edward came to Doncaster in 1322 and, by all accounts, spent a great deal of time here as well as visiting Bentley in August. He reputedly healed 72 people of their

afflictions just by touching them. Unfortunately for Edward, he was cruelly murdered at the age of 43. I will not dwell on the method used to kill him only to say that it involved a red hot iron, bowels, and screams that were heard as far off as the Castle, I will leave the rest up to your imagination!

During the time of Fledburgh, French gate was also known as Franksyk gate. The street was narrow with open gutters, domestic comforts and sanitary requirements were utterly disregarded, any pestilence that occured as a result of this poor and unhealthy sanitation was regarded as a curse from God as a reward for bad behaviour. French gate became the accepted name for the street from around 1715. At this time the river Cheswold and the green fields were easily accessible at several points. As time went on and land was bought up and built upon, access to these "pleasant footpaths and cheerful by-roads" was near on impossible as the routes to the open spaces were either blocked or obstructed by the selfish owners or occupiers.

There was a 'rus in urbe' (countryside in the town) feel to the area during the 1300's as the houses were built cheek to cheek with orchards, vegetable gardens, paddocks, and green fields laid out and preserved. The social hub would have been the 13th century Early English style parish church of St. George.

Over 500 years later the landscape was much the same. To the rear of the properties on the street there was a multitude of orchards, and "in the spring it was fragranced with sweet blossoms". Mr John Whitaker, a house owner in the 1880's "delighted in his garden" and his grounds were extremely sought after at the later property sale. The street was one of two halves, French gate east and French gate west. Below is a full list of the residents as of 1760:

French Gate East

- Mr John Ward – house and orchard
- Hannah Willis
- William France
- William Lacey
- Mrs Wainman, for widow husband
- John Battie
- Barbara Bennett
- Mrs Wainman, for Jonathan Lacey
- Mrs Wainman, for Wiiliam Hague
- Mrs Wainman, for William Marsh
- Stephen Radley
- Widow Bolton – two tenements
- Widow Bolton, for another tenement
- Mr Abbey, late Mrs Wagstaff and other tenements
- Mr Abbey, for Mrs Patrick – house

- Mr Thomas Malin
- Robert Oxley
- Mr Taylor
- Mrs Neal
- Late Isaac Husband
- Mrs France, for Barratts house
- Mrs France, for Joshua Brooke
- Mrs France, for late Newbold
- Mrs France, for late Joseph Denton
- John Tootal
- Widow Killinglock
- Thomas Farmott
- Thomas Parker
- Charles Williams
- Jonathan Stansfield
- Jonathan Jennings
- Late Goldthorp
- Thomas Green
- Mrs Rickard, for Jenkinson
- Mrs Abbey – house
- Jonathan Kay
- James Major
- Mr Hague – house, stables, and coach-house
- Jonathan Oldfield
- Mrs Pugh – house
- Mrs Pugh, for Mr Creakhill
- Mrs Pugh, for William Penny
- Mrs Pugh, for Robinson
- Mrs Pugh, for Edward Ravenhill
- Mrs Pugh, for now John Butlers shop and stable
- Mr Isaac Smith – new house
- Mr Isaac Smith – old house (John Smith tenant)
- Thomas Norton, for late John Ince
- Mr William Siddal
- Mr Middleton
- Mr Alderman Whitaker
- Mrs France, for Joshua Brooke
- Mrs France, for John Oxley

- Thomas Brown
- Joshua Dixon – house and kiln
- Mrs Wade – house
- Mr John Watson
- Mr John Watson, for late Swallow
- Mr John Watson, for Carter
- Lancelot Dickinson
- Mr Halifax
- Mr Bingley
- Mr Godfrey Washington
- Mr Alderman Malin
- Mr Gill
- William Stanley
- John Oxley
- Mr Thomas Atkinson
- Martha Lane

French Gate West

- Mr William Aldam – house
- Mr Willim Aldam, for Mrs Beal
- Mrs Sunderland
- Late Mr Inman
- Mr Tomlinson
- Miss Rodwell
- Mr Sheppard
- Mr Farrer
- Mr Inman
- James Bailes
- Mr Alderman Whitaker – stable and barn
- Mr Alderman Whitaker, for Wakefield
- Mr Benjamin Elston – house
- Mr Charles Mitchell – house
- Jonathan Smith
- Mr Thomas Hoult, for late Gamble
- Charles Mitchel, for Mrs Maud
- Charles Mitchel, for Joseph Morley

- Charles Mitchel, for one other
- Mr Gill, Jnr
- Mr Holmes, Jnr
- Mr Wildsmith – barn and stable
- Mr Hawley – two stables
- Jonathan Watson, for late Mr Pheazant's shop
- David Richards – house
- Late Smith and Dobson
- Thomas Grant
- Jonathan Watson, for Joshua Brooks and George Ashmoor
- Jonathan Watson, for Jonathan Allen and William Mitchel
- Jonathan Watson, for Thomas Misdale and Thomas Mapplebeck
- Mr Hawley – house
- Francis Squires – stable at the bottom of Common lane
- Francis Squires – cellar
- Mr Wildsmith – house
- Thomas Mapplebeck and tenements
- Alderman Hancock
- Mr Hallowell
- Mrs Scamadine
- Jonathan Goldthorpe – two tenements
- Jonathan Whaley – house
- Thomas White – and tenements
- Late John Gayforth – and tenements
- Thomas White – house
- Richard Thomas – water engine
- Charles Mitchell, for Mrs Mawhood
- Charles Mitchell, for Joshua Morley

The Future (as of 91 years ago)

91 years ago in 1921 Ernest Phillips, the editor of the Doncaster Chronicle newspaper speculated on the future of

the town. The following article is some of his predictions. Did he get it right? Let's see:

"Doncaster is ever changing. Unlike some old towns – Chester, Lancaster, York – it retains none of its mediaeval characteristics. It is essentially modern. It has been built and rebuilt times without number. It is now undergoing its greatest change.

For centuries it was a quiet market town. There was no bustle and clang of commerce, no feverish race for wealth in industry. The smoke of Sheffield and the activity of Leeds seemed a long way off. At the beginning of the last century (early 1800), Doncaster was described as one of the handsomest residential towns in the whole of England. The massive houses, Hall Gate, Priory Place, and a few other thoroughfares testified that it was a town where well-to-do families loved to take life easily and placidly.

A change has now come over the scene. Doncaster is destined to be the centre of a great and rich industry. The base of this country's industrial greatness is coal. Wherever you find coal, there you find trade and industry active – iron

and steel works, cotton and woollen mills, engineering shops, and the hundred and one manifestations of our national genius for making things.

There is coal all around Doncaster and, in fact, under Doncaster as well. There is coal under the racecourse, there is coal under the corporation reservoir at Thrybergh. It stretches right to the East Coast, dipping deeper and deeper, til it reaches a depth where it is unworkable. But it is workable all around Doncaster, and this has led to a remarkable development during the last 15 years (since 1906). Over half a dozen new coal-pits have been sunk and are now working daily. The nearest to Doncaster is at Bentley, scarce 3 miles away. Others are at Carcroft, Askern, Woodlands, Edlington, Rossington, Hatfield, Thorne, etc., and others are in contemplation at Armthorpe, Finningly, and elsewhere.

The result of this is that a network of villages are springing up around the town. A modern colliery gives employment to 2 or 3 thousand hands. It raises 2 or 3 thousand tons of coal each day. Some of them, like the one at Hickleton, only about 7 miles out of Doncaster, raise even 4,000 tons per day. A village springs up. It houses 5 or 6 thousand folk. A new church is erected, chapels and schools are reared, shops and picture-houses and clubs appear almost by magic; and lo, where a year ago you had a sleepy hamlet, now you have a throbbing industrial town, with a rattle of railway wagons, the clang of pit head gear, and all the usual features of town life.

 These new centres look to Doncaster. They are linked up by means of the electric tram car. They come into town and do a great deal of their shopping. Thus the town benefits, and one result already is seen in the newly built shops which adorn our streets. Our theatres, our music halls, our public institutions, all benefit by these new populations which now cover what was once the sparsely populated countryside.

But this is not all. Where there is coal there is other trade, and so we find that other industries are coming to Doncaster. Before the coal boom of the last few years, Doncaster could not be called a manufacturing town. True, there was the large establishment of the Great Northern Railway, where anything can be made from a handcart to an express locomotive; and, in addition, there were brass and wire works, etc.

But the working of the new coalfield will change, and is changing, all this. Just outside Doncaster, at Sandall, a mere hamlet on the river bank, a Lancashire glass-making firm are making a factory to find work for 5,000 employees; they will construct a model village, with a church and club and library. Another Lancashire firm of woollen manufacturers are coming to Bentley, even nearer than Sandall, and they will build a large works for the manufacture of their own specialities. Further away, at Finningley, a Sheffield firm is building a vast place wherein to make motor cars.

In short, Doncaster is on the eve of a great development. At least half a dozen firms have come or are coming into the town. Others are making enquiries for land. The selection of Doncaster is due to several facts that give the town an advantage. It is not only on the main line of the Great Northern Railway, but 6 other railways have running power into Doncaster. Moreover, the canal which runs through Doncaster on its way from Sheffield to Goole and Hull, not only links us up with Sheffield, but gives us direct access to the sea. If this canal is widened and deepened, and made a real ship canal, as it almost certainly will be in the not too distant future, its value to the trade of the town will be greatly increased.

To make a modern manufacturing town, there are several essentials. The first and greatest is coal. Doncaster is not only the centre of the newest but the richest coalfield in Great Britain. It is true that it is a great depth. Some of the new pits are over 900 yards deep, more than half a mile; but modern engineering skill has overcome the difficulties of getting coal at that enormous depth. Powerful fans drive fresh air from above down one shaft, and after it has circulated through all the galleries it is sucked up another shaft. Engines nowadays can be made strong enough to draw coal to the bank from almost any depth.

Thus the manufacturer has plenty of coal at Doncaster. The coal merchant has seven railways and a canal at his service if he wants to sell it or ship it to a country across the sea. Doncaster, therefore, is in a good position to make headway; and while some enthusiasts think the town may some day be a second leeds or Sheffield, there are others who think its greatest developments will be its coal trade, and that it may be in a few years time a second Cardiff as a coal distributing centre.

These things, however, are in the future. How soon they may be upon us, none may say; but that the town is changing every day is a certainty. Within the last 12 years nearly ten new pits have been opened; half a dozen new branch railway lines have been constructed; at least three or more model villages have been planned; four or five new churches have been erected and consecrated. Tramway lines have been extended from the town to three colliery villages, and the Corporation has projects for others.

The probability is that Doncaster in a generation will have completely changed its character. Its rural aspect will have gone. It will be a busy manufacturing town. A ring of coal mines will encircle it. Iron works, glass works, woollen mills, engineering shops will stand where now the farm lad drives his team and the ploughshare furrows the loam. The canal will bear on its bosom the products of mine and mill on their way to coastal ports for shipment over the seas.

The town itself will change. The last remnants of old Doncaster – in such narrow thoroughfares as Scot Lane – will disappear. Broad streets will be the rule. The tramcars will link up with every outside centre of life and trade. There will be little left to remind the visitor that he stands within one of the oldest boroughs of England – a town of Roman foundation, a borough that has lived its life in all the succeeding ages of Saxon and Dane and Norman lordship; that has echoed to the tramp of Roman Legions; that has seen Saxon and Norman at deadly grips; that has emerged out of feudal darkness into the fierce white light of 20th century civilization.

It is in order that the story of the coloured pageant of our past may be imprinted on the mind of young Doncaster that this [piece] is written – that in regarding the present and speculating about the future, we may not be unmindful of a past which comes down to us as a very precious heritage.

Published by ©Doncaster History publishing 2012.

DONCASTER HISTORY

10462521R00025

Printed in Great Britain
by Amazon.co.uk, Ltd.,
Marston Gate.